A Poetic Book on Relationships

Love
IS A
DOUBLE-EDGED SWORD

MARK McCAULEY

Inquiries and Book Orders should be addressed to:

Great Writers Media
Email: info@greatwritersmedia.com
Phone: (302) 918-5570

ISBN: 978-1-956517-53-8 (sc)
ISBN: 978-1-956517-54-5 (ebk)

Rev 10/27/2021

Contents

Dedicated to the inspirational of love

$\mathcal{P}$reface

Love is so vast that there is no end to this subject; however, it has a beginning, the roots to where true love lies. Each stem of the root is a level of degree by which love can agree. The depth of love is the fountain of wells where the source of love is drawn. Love for a friend, Love of a sibling, a parent's love, cross-cultural love, inter-racial love, etc. are various loves. Each portrays the feelings of love.

This poetic book focuses on the love within relationships; the relationship between a woman and a man. The agony, pain, hurts, joy, pleasures, the feelings of butterflies, the stress, headaches, heart-aches, etc. that the feeling of love brings.

In this poetic book on relationships I teach love through our everyday feelings by exploring our consciousness and examining these tem-poral feelings that often sway us. The area by which this poetic love book speaks is the five key areas of love, which are (1) the pain of love (the love that makes you cry), (2) the art of love (enjoying good sex), romance (flowers, cards and candy), (4) aesthetic (beautiful, beauty), and (5) the inspirational love (God kind of love or spiri-tual love), which is the strength to any love. Absence of any one of these five principles is the beginning of an unbalanced relationship where there is a need being neglected, which will result in confu-sion, improper love, unwanted love, separation, etc.

Chapter 1

What Is Love?

What Is Love?

I used to believe that love was an uncontrollable feeling that comes and goes when it wants. Now I believe love is the sacrifice of self to benefit others. I used to believe that love was sex. Now I believe sex is the art of expressing love through body contact what the mouth can't utter. I used to believe that true love was found. Now I believe love is a relationship built by two people. Love is never found; if it were love it wouldn't have been lost. I used to believe that love was lust. Now I know that lust is the sexual gratification, often disguised as love to benefit self at the expense of others.

What then is love? Love is a built relationship. Love is the total knowledge one has of self and their mate; one cannot love what they don't know, because love is a choice based on commitment, not feelings, for feelings will sway you.

Once one is conscious of the true meaning of love, they elevate their love to its optimal level, where love becomes unconditional; the highest level, where the sacred vows take a stand, through death do we part.

Various Feelings

Feelings are unstable emotions that bring joy and pain. Feelings are strong forces within a soul; each force has a taste. Sexual feelings are the appetite of a delightful taste; they soothes the soul and mellows the mind with unspeakable pleasures. Rejections of one's love are the painful feelings in one's heart, when feelings of despair become a ruling force within one's soul. Feelings are desires of wants or needs in a particular moment; the eagerness of these sudden urges are what we call various feelings.

Love Stalker

Beware of those who come around with warm greetings and half smiles. Every smile is with intent; a sudden hello is accompanied with a hidden motive. It was her looks that caught my attention; the scent of fragrance, the gleam in her eyes, that captured my soul. I fastened my eyes on her as I watched her from afar, admiring the splendor of her beauty. When she walked, I walked; when she smiled, I smiled; when she laughed, I laughed; secretly lurked as I stood in the shadows admiring her every move. I predicted our destiny and told myself one day she will be mine. To bring this déjà vu to pass, I went and sat next to her favorite spot, under the fig tree where the fresh breeze of the sea cooled my heart. Reading the same book she was reading, I hoped this would create the coincidence to befriend her with the motive of capturing her heart. She talked and talked, confirming all the things I observed about her. We became close, even to the point of matching when we met under the fig tree, where she often picked the ripe fruit for me. At times we would take turns reading to each other. This particular moment my head was resting on her lap while I gazed at the sky, while she read. Her voice was soothing; it was music to my ears and melody to my heart. The bond I felt every time she would read to me, was like a parent reading a bedtime story to their child. Just as he slept the parent would give a good night kiss and turn the lights off. While looking at the sky I noticed the sun going down, and to my surprise I felt a soft, soft, soft kiss to my lips that melted my heart. She read a note hidden with the pages of her book. The law of togetherness states the more time you spent together, the more likely you will be together. How can two people spend so much time together and not feel for each other? I returned her kiss and gently told her today you have made my hidden desires a reality, and from this day on, you will be mine forever.

The Love in One Friendship

To have a friend that you like and they don't know is a painful feeling. These feelings I have for you started all those nights you came to me hurt, confused, crying, needing a friend to talk to, someone to encourage you in your moment of despair. As I understood your feelings, I felt your pains—not realizing that I was falling for you. Suddenly, I realized when you hurt, I hurt, when you cry, my heart weeps.

The constant thoughts of being with you always numb the painful feelings I often feel for you. I'm feeling more than friendship. To tell her, I don't know how. I don't want to take the chance of losing this friendship. So I wait till the next time she comes running to me crying. I won't open the door, that's my heart. Just to make you realize the painful feeling that one day I won't be there for you. Then you would understand my feelings and you will feel the same way and love will carry us on.

Blind Love

Love has no color; love is neither black or white, but can be hot or cold. Love knows no age; therefore love does not age. Love transcends time. Love is not a respecter of persons, which means love does not discriminate. Love is the meaning you give it. Love cannot be restricted; the confinement of love is the boundaries the two set, to tame the feeling of love. Love is priceless, cannot be bought or sold, for its worth is far more than gold. It's free upon agreement, with the promise of proper care. Love is the essence of time; the time I had with you were the moments I loved you the most. It was then and only then I was able to express my love for you.

Flood of the Heart

The frown on her face; the redness of her eyes, are the dark clouds that position themselves in front of the sun. The sounds of thunder and lightning are catastrophic of one's external pain. As I wipe away the first teardrop, then the sudden falls of raindrops. It's raining in my heart; my heart is flooded; the world that I had with you is no more; the flood has destroyed everything. Love is painful when the rain in one's heart won't stop falling; forty days and forty nights it rained. I cried my last cry; I took my last punches. My heart is flooded with your tears; no souls could survive this flood. I was forced through pain to drown all memories and uproot all feelings of this wicked and abusive love. On the fortieth day the rain stopped. My heart began to dry, which took another forty days of finding myself. The sudden smiles were the sunshine that now lights my heart. I feel free; I feel like a new person, soaring in the air. I will open my eyes to a new day, not realizing I couldn't open my eyes, because I didn't survive the flood.

Love

Love is like a sea; the deeper you get into it the harder it is to get out. The longer you stay the easier it is not to want to leave. And if you do want to leave, by the time you realize it you can't leave. Because that time you're in too deep. You've adjusted to it and it's killing you without you knowing it. You can't see the harm it's doing to you but if you don't wake up you'll end up hurt. You'll end up hurt; you'll drown; love is killing you.

By Nerissa McCauley

Paranoid

How do you know when you're in love? When you hear his voice and you smile; when his laughter brings you joy and his pain brings you sorrow. When he makes you forget all your problems and he then becomes your problem. He can no longer fix the rest. A day without him brings you down; you begin to over think comments, meaningless comments. All because he's too good. It seems inevitable that something will go wrong. You try to prevent it. You make false accusations when in reality you're bringing your worst fear to life. Destroying all you've built. You start to obsess, but thinking about him can lead to so much anger, joy, confusion, obsession, all at the same time. You're blind-sided by love. Things become invisible to you; nothing matters; you focus on him. Day and night poison your mind with thoughts of him. You blackout, pass hours… days, time wasted. Just thinking of him, wondering if what you're feeling is real. Wondering if he feels the same about you. You want him to feel how you feel when you're away from him…incomplete. You want him to want you the way you want him. You're hoping his I love yous are as real as yours. Hoping what you have will never end. Something tells you not to get your hopes up, to move on. But maybe you're just paranoid.

By Nerissa McCauley

Chapter 2

Love Is Pain

This Is the Last Time

Have you ever been so hurt that you said to yourself, "this is the last time"? Have you ever been so sad that being mad wouldn't have made a different? I was one who was hurt by love. Wounded for loving the wrong woman. Slain like a mouse caught in a trap. It's painful; so painful that my heart is numb. Never again, never again. This is the last time.

I've been slain by the only person I trusted. If love was a crime, she is guilty of murder. No one wants to hear my pain; it's of no gain. I'm dying inside. No one could charge her; there is no evidence. My evidence is my bleeding heart, which no one sees. Who can undo this pain? Who can unnumb this heart of mine? Never again, never again, this is the last time.

Do birds fall in love? Do birds get hurt? Why then is their song so sweet? Is it because they have no feelings? But they bleed, which means they feel. Well I'm human, and I have feelings; it hurts. No sweet song could mend this broken heart of mine. No sweet song can cheer me up. Never again, never again, this is the last time.

Love Is a Double-Edged Sword

Tears of pain resulting from harsh words that pierce the soul. Some use words as a sword to cut through one's heart. The sharpness of words are the sword drawn out of the mouth of fools. When the sword, which is meant to protect, is turned, aiming at the heart of the one you love, the thrust of vehement words goes into the fragile heart of a helpless mate. As she turns in silence to hide the flow of bitter water that consumes her eyes, she closes her eyes to quickly, shuts the gate against the flood that now drowns her heart.

As I watch the tears drip on the cheeks of my love's face, seeing the tearing of her heart and the pain it causes her, I feel remorseful and I silence my mouth to hear my heart speak. I close my eyes to shut in the tears that are building up—for men don't cry, echoing the thoughts of my forefather. I desperately search for kind words to dull this sharp sword that now divides us. Kind words will change the countenance of her face, from the frown of sadness to the brightness of her sunny smile. Constructive words will build and edify her, building back her self-esteem. The kind of words that will nurse her tender heart as a mother nurses their child when wounded. Following the directions of my heart, I extend my hand to her soft, delicate face, gently caressing her cheeks, wiping away her tears with the strokes of my thumb, as I muster up inner strength to softly say sorry, and in utterance I whisper the words of assurance and say I love you.

Cancerous Love

At times, there are illnesses that creep up from nowhere, showing little or no symptoms. If it goes unnoticed or untreated it would lead to disease. Headaches, heartaches, heartbreak are various symptoms of a wounded love. Although not fatal, if not treated would lead to cancerous love, the deadliest of all illnesses. The early detection of this deadly dis-ease is separation, when two cells that are one part ways, causing one cell to fall apart or deteriorate, for lack of ability to go on. At this stage, the only cure or remedy for this fatal illness is to bring the two souls back together.

I rushed through the emergency room, only to see the woman I once loved. As I approached the room where my love lay, I saw families and friends standing by, eagerly waiting, hoping for good news. While waiting, I felt the coldness of those who blamed me, saying to themselves only if he would have stayed with her. While contending with these thoughts, the doctor silently approached, and said sorry, cancerous love is what acid does to the body; it eats away one's soul.

Dying Love

Most of us have a secret place somewhere deep within our heart and soul. A place where we go to sort things through, when feelings of love become overwhelmed with pain. This place is thoughts of imagination, memories of imagery, and reflections of moments of being together. This place of isolation and loneliness is the secret place we go to bury feelings of those we love, or set on fire all images of thought of those we truly love. This hidden place is the secret darkness of the heart and the soul where no one knows the murders which are committed, only she who commits them. I've been dragged to this hidden place by a love which I thought was true. The heart of this woman is where I now lay. Helplessly wounded by reason of separation as she watches my dying love.

Trapped in Time

The minute I saw you, at that very hour I knew that one day we would be together forever. As our friendship grew, so did my feelings for you, reaching to the point of no return. How can this be? How could I love you, knowing that it is wrong, for I'm already bound by vow to the youth of my companion.

Falling in love is an uncontrollable feeling, a feeling that comes and goes. A painful feeling that pierces the soul. A hurtful feeling when one refuses to succumb to the object of their desires. I'm lost in love, trapped in a vicious cycle called time, where minutes become hours and every hour becomes a day when the days seem endless. As the clock ticks so does my heart beat, echoing every minutes, hour and endless days of me longing for you.

Scorned

Scars of the heart are the wounds in one's mind. Often, reflection of this hurt is the fearfulness of falling again. When love hurts so much, it leaves you scorned.

Falling, but Didn't Fall

Marriage is the union of two souls; commitments are the vows the two take. For better and for worst through death do us part, is the foundation of a lasting love. When feelings begin to develop and the one who is committed is falling in love with another soul, what is one to do? I contemplated suicide on abandoning my vows. Should I give in to my feelings or should I suffer the pain and torture that this new feeling of love brings? This is a sacrifice one will have to make. Not until one understands, will he make the right choice.

As I thought on my feelings, feelings are temporary emotions that inflict the soul, which generate desires and passions, causing heartburn which are the wounds in one's heart. But in time, it will heal. One must master his feelings or will be forever tossed to and fro as the wind does the leaves when fallen to the ground, leaving a trail of unstable love. One must realize that falling in love is inevitable, and it is only wrong when one has given in to their feelings, rendering them to fall.

How long does one keep falling? As long as one does not give in to the feeling of temptation. This realization only comes to those who are committed and have experienced the temptation of falling in love with another, but have not fallen by reason of the vows one has taken.

Love Hurt

Love is the feeling one person feels for another. These feelings are strong emotions that take control of your mind, causing you to meditate on this person all day. The thought of seeing or hearing her voice lessens the hurt. So I phoned. I called and called, numerous times, only desiring to hear the voice of this woman who holds my mind captive, whose love I yearned to touch, so I could be free. No answer as the pain is intensified; suddenly I heard the voice of the operator in my head saying the person you're trying to call is either not home or is busy getting her groove on. Ignoring these thoughts, I hung the phoned up, as I asked myself where could she be, is she ignoring my love for fear of falling in love which comes with pain? The pain I feel for her cannot fully express how much I long to be with her. Desiring her with passion, I went and lay down, hoping I could sleep off some of this hurt, holding the pillow tight, crouching down, folding myself in half, like someone who holds their stomach when it hurts, as I endured the hurt of this love.

Sometimes I Wonder

Sometimes I wonder, why is it that I love you? Or is it even love? Is it infatuation? Puppy love, I want it to be love. But sometimes I wonder, I wonder if I can live without you or will I sulk for a week until the next "Love of my life"? I wonder but I don't want to find out. I never want to lose you. I don't want to experience life without you. I don't want to cry myself to sleep night after night. I dread waking up day after day. I want to wake up happy, awaiting your voice. I want sleepless nights thinking of you.

By Nerissa McCauley

Lost

I remember when you told me you loved me. You said we would be together forever. But now you're gone, leaving me bewildered. I'm lost without you, lost in some kind of imaginary world. In my head you never left me. In my head you're still here, but I know you left me. Who will rescue me? Rescue me from the heartache; the pain that comes attached to love. It's slowly breaking me, leaving me lost in a world of love. When did forever end?

By Nerissa McCauley

Chapter 3

Aesthetics

Are You an Angel?

Last night as I slept, you or an angel came to me in my dream, couldn't tell difference. You had a long white gown that fitted your body so right. Your beauty cast a glow upon my room, that my heart also felt the radiance of your love. I stood in awe, looking into your mysterious eyes. I became mesmerized for I saw your soul, your thoughts of me; love of passion, filled with pain, burning desires which could only be quenched if you were not forbidden. She flutters her wings as to fly away. I quickly hold her hand and embrace her soft, delicate body with a hug that melted my soul.

In the stillness of the night while holding her so tight, the thoughts of letting her go were dreadful. As she unwrapped her arms from around me, she whispered wondrous things in my ear which will remain untold. As I turned to kiss her, she disappeared. Fearful of the sorrow that my love she would not take, not wanting to awake, I thought to myself, can a mortal man fall in love with an angel?

So Beautiful

It is often said that beauty is in the eyes of the beholder. You are the beauty every man desires to behold. I, myself, once had that desire until we became friends. When I first saw you, I said to myself, wow she is truly beautiful, so beautiful that the brightness of her smile could make a blind man see. As I left your presence, I again thought to myself, who is loving you? What mortal man has the benefit of enjoying your presence? What lucky man has captured your heart, and does he know how fortunate he is? For a girl like you is the angel which men dream about. What man will not war over you? If I were a king, I'd give you a throne and make you my queen. I will even give my kingdom to the lucky man that has captured your heart in exchange for your love. Your precious eyes that sparkle within your face, your smile which causes me to blush. You are a unique creature, fearfully and wonderfully made. You're so beautiful.

My Wife

Today is the day. Today marks the ending of my life. Today marks the beginning of a new life with you. On this day, I vow to look only at you. On this day, I proposed to you, kneeling on one knee, extending my hand to you, asking you to take this diamond ring as a small token of my love for you. And let this token be a symbol of my love around your finger. Today I declare to you and before all witnesses that I will fulfill all your needs. On this day, I promise to secure and cherish you. On this day, I say I do. We will share a home; we will share one bed. Everything we do, we will do it together. We will always be in agreement. Having one mind, one heart and one soul. We will be one. Nothing can separate us, because what God has joined together, no man can separate. Today, I ask you to be my Wife.

My True Love

Love is good when everything else is going good. Love is a high that takes you beyond the clouds. Until one day that cloud turns into rain, bringing you low.

True love now becomes the meaning of love when two souls stand the test of time. The storms of life are the trials of love; endurance is the hope that love will last. The pain of love is the gain that true love has been proven when it's stood the test of time.

Shadows

Beautiful women are shadows in one's mind. For they leave imprints in one's soul. Shadows are dark spirits whose reflection is often seen on the wall. Spirits are thoughts, the projected image in one's mind. This is a plague called the art of aesthetic. At night, thoughts of you often invoke your presence; suddenly I found myself in your world talking with you, holding and kissing you until someone turned the lights on and you quickly vanished. During the day I daydream, thinking whether these thoughts are real. At night your image consumes me.

My mind sees things no one sees. This illusion is the shadow cast upon me; by one stare, I found myself in constant thoughts of you. Shadows are the illusion of one's desires, the intangible things we hope for, the enigma of dark hidden thoughts.

Black Woman

Brown and nestle is the beauty of this young lady. Her flavor is what I favor. Black woman is what I call her, for her taste warms my inside. Black woman, your wisdom is able to make a fool wise; your knowledge is the key to success, and your understanding is what makes sense out of me. Your strength is more than ten thousand armies who seek to chain and enslave you. Yet you overcome them with your love. As you walk through this world with humility, demonstrating your inner beauty, your outer beauty is the sparkle in a diamond. The attraction you bring is what makes the guys buzz around you like you're some sweet honey. Your natural looks and beautiful face upset the makeup artist. Your soft, beautiful complexion is what gave birth to the suntan. Your beautiful thick lick lips, full of juices, it makes me thirst; always longing to be with you. Your legs so beautiful and shiny; if every girl had legs like yours, stockings would go out of business. Your slim waist and big breasts are what men desire. Black woman, this is why I love you, you're naturally beautiful, for you are created by God.

Beauty

What is beauty, what is beautiful, what is the difference? There's two types of beauty. One comes from within and the other is the outward appearance. Spiritual attraction is the beauty that comes from within. It looks beyond the physical and expresses its beauty through love and kindness. Beauty that comes from within makes one happy. Physical attraction tends to only look at the appearance or is first impression, and is often expressed through lust. Physical beauty never seeks to understand you or take time to see the inside. All and all, beauty is not beauty unless it's beautiful. It's often said, beauty is in the eyes of the beholder. But I say beauty is the act of expressing love and kindness. One might say beauty is skin-deep. But I say it is the expression of one's uniqueness. Are you beautiful or do you have beauty, what's the difference? Beauty that comes within is the beauty that is beautiful.

Chapter 4

The Art of Love

If I Were You

If I were a plane, I'd fly you around the world, showing the finest things in life. If I were a car I'd drive you crazy, guaranteeing you pleasure night after night. If I were a house, I'd let you in, sheltering you from the stormy weather that is so boisterous. If I were a horse, I'd give you the cover that firmly fit over the saddle, and let you ride me all night long. If I were a bird I'd bring you to my nest and sing sweet songs to you that would chirp away all your pain, easing your mind. If I were you, I'd give this romance a chance.

The One

To everyone, I found someone who is one of a kind, 'cause she's kinda like me. She's different and unique. She's not loose, like some girls; she's tight like the tie on one's neck. She's saving herself for that special one, for she fears God. Her vision is what gave me sight. Insight to a strong woman's love. A woman of courage and strength, she's what one would call a virtuous woman. Thugs cannot game her, 'cause she doesn't play games. If insisted she would send you playing scrabble.

She doesn't fall for soft whispers of sweet nothings, 'cause I'm her sweet something. Let it be known to all my exes, sorry for all my empty promises, the pain I caused. I ask your forgiveness, so I will be free of the feeling of guilt, for I now know what it feels like to be in love. Release me, oh foolish woman, and forgive me, then I shall tell you the secrets to my commitment. Fear God and keep your legs closed and whomsoever you're with will commit; then and only then will they appreciate your mind or soul and not only your body. Let it be known to all my homeys that you respect this woman with the highest regard, 'cause how you treat her is how you treat me; for she is going to bear my name, 'cause she's the one.

My Soul Mate

The soul is the mind of a person that displays emotions, where choices are made. A mate is the companion of a soul which one dates. Feelings of love are the mutual agreement that is felt. Wanting to be alone in a secret place. This sacred place is the dark, quiet lace where no one is supposed to see the nakedness of these souls. Where the expressions of love begins. Fondling, wet kisses, and constant caressing are the expressing of deeply rooted feelings that now start to surface. The art of love is the activity that happens in this sacred place. Where sexual gratification is the climax that one has maximized. Soul mate now become the agreed place where the two souls mate.

Chapter 5

Inspirational

God's Love

True love comes from God, for God is love; in order for anyone to know love they must know Jesus Christ, for he is the epitome of love.

Love Is a Sacrifice

Adam's love for his wife caused him to eat the fruit she picked for him. Eve's love for knowledge caused her to eat the forbidden fruit. Jesus' love for us caused him to sacrifice his life by dying for our sins.

Love Is Knowledge

True love comes from God. One cannot truly love unless they have been loved by God. Then will they know how to love themselves and others. Love is knowing; knowledge is the key to understanding love.

Obedience Is Love

God made man to love him. God made woman to love the man. God gave children to woman to love them. When children obey their parents it shows they love them. When the wife obeys her husband it shows she loves him. When man obeys God it shows that he loves his maker. God loves us by providing, protecting and healing us. Man loves his wife by providing, protecting and caring for his wife. Woman loves her children by providing, protecting and nursing them. Obedience is the fruit of love.

Love Never Dies

True love never dies; true love lives on and on. When the souls of two loves have been severed by confusion, mistrust, unforgiveness, bitterness, etc., separation is now the peaceful state where true love lies dormant.

Resurrected Love

There are only two remedies to bring back a dead love: a changed character and a willing mind.

Integrity

A child left alone will shame his parents. So will every Christian who does not walk in integrity, they shame their maker.

Life

Your love is like the air around me. The air I breathe is what gives me life. If you take your love from me I will die.

Mirror

As the door closed, a voice said to me, look around and tell me what you see. I said to myself, I see people all around me from all walks of life; sad faces, happy faces, some sitting, some standing holding on, while other are reading , talking, laughing, joking, listening to their walkman; some even look puzzled while some are in deep thoughts, each one in their own world.

The voice said to me, look around and tell me what you see. I said to myself, I see pictures, posters, advertisements, etc. As the door closed and we headed through the tunnel, the voice said to me, look around and tell me what you see. I just happened to look at the window through the dark tunnel and I saw myself in the window. So I said to myself, I see me. The voice said to me, you see he who speaks to you. You see a reflection of me in your image. As my stop approached, the voice then said to me, write this down, mirror is a reflection of your current state of mind whose image you portray.

Lesson from My Past

What is love? This is the question every man and woman ought to ask themselves. So I ask myself this question by reflecting back to my many relationships. As I journey through time, memories of past loves consume my mind; feelings of despair, shattered dreams, broken promises and forgotten hopes were the bitterness that saturated my soul. As I travel in thought, down the streets of memory lane, suddenly scenes flash before me as I observe and admire the beauty of this teenage couple. The pureness and innocence of this love, one could assume it was forever. Now I know the reason she broke my heart, it was her parents who encouraged it. So devastated was I that I promised myself never to fall in love again; this was Pamela, my first love.

As I turn to walk, another scene flashes before me, and I see a young, beautiful couple sitting in the park talking. As I observe, admiring the uniqueness of this relationship, also the weaknesses of this young guy; he was very unfaithful, controlled by his lust and passion for girls. For the first time, I saw the sleepless nights, constant cries, hurts and pain this young girl went through, by reasons of his lies and unfaithfulness. This was Michelle, my second love. I was saddened by this scene as it brought tears to my eyes. Before I could wipe my eyes, another scene flashed before me; this time the scene was rapid, each scene conveying a message.

The last scene was Roni, my seventh love. As the thoughts slowly drifted, sleepiness faded from my eyes, I was awakened only to hear the quietness of the night. I quietly got up from my bed, not wanting to wake the woman who lay next to me. I made my way to the terrace, looking up at the night sky. The stars were so bright and shining while I thought on the vision and its messages. Dreams are the revealment of one's past; dreams are the solution to one's future. Fear engulfed me as I saw the patterns of my live. The trail of shattered dreams, broken promises and forgotten hopes was the theme of my life, motivated my lust in the absence of love. I was afraid of losing the woman who lays in my bed whose love soothes my soul. So I asked myself, what is love? Then I heard the voice of the Lord saying I am love; seek me and you will know me for I am love. I fell on my knees and started to pray. When I finished, I heard the wisdom of the Lord teaching me love through my past, saying, Knowledge of me is the beginning of love. Love is what determines right from wrong. Love is the ability to forgive and forget. Love is the self-sacrifice one makes. Love is based on commitment, never on feelings, for feelings would mislead you. Love is the total acceptance of body, soul and spirit, which will consummate your soul mate. Love is wisdom based on wise decisions. Whatever is not understood will be misused or abused. What you don't know is what will kill you. In your situation you didn't realize that when you said you'd never love again you immersed yourself within the spirit of lust, which shielded your heart and protected your feelings by assassinating all your relationships, those who came close to your heart.

So I confessed aloud that I loved this woman, as I felt within my heart a feeling of heaviness departing from my heart and a child-like love nursing my heart. I quiet walked to my room where my love lay, sound asleep. I gently kissed her on her forehead and whispered, "I love you," for today the Lord has taught me love.

Girlstar

It's Friday night, just got paid, I'm heading to the strip club for solo. Hoping Girlstar will be there. A girl I met last year with the fellers, who only wants to dance with me when I'm there. Who promises me that If I give her a chance she will stand by me forever. As she would say, "I got your back, boo." Not long I fell head over heels for her. For she is special, she is beautiful, well shaped and boy could she dance, her sex game was encore, nothing but the bliss of satisfaction. She did me right, I had no complaints. Always came through when my funds were low. When I'm around her I feel illumination, she makes me feel like a real man, a good man. Girlstar, I love you, you're my boo. Until one day we had our last fight which brought me to tears. For the first time I was contemplating leaving her. I went to the park to find a place of solitude. A place where I could be alone. The only thing I wanted to hear was birds chirping and the sounds of nature in the night breeze. In the quietness it dawned on me that the only time she goes to the club is to make up for my insufficient funds, when the bills are due. I fell asleep, began to dream.

Under the fig tree I sat, gazing into the night sky. As I start to count the stars, the cloud moving will block my count, making me lose count. The brightness of this particular star caught my attention. As if it was telepathically speaking to me. Questioning me, am I only visible at night? Do I stop shining during the day? Or do you perceive me as a light switch that could be turned off and on. Pondering on these thoughts challenged my sleep. As it dawned on me, stars always shine no matter the day, hour or the seasons. Stars will always be bright no matter the condition or circumstances. Stars are the light that guides us through the night, leading us to the day. I realize, Girlstar was always there; during my darkest hours she was the one holding it down. She was the star in my darkness.

Painful Pleasure

Sex is pain, but pleasurable. Pain without pleasure is rape.

All Day

Just to make the day long, I stop the sun from going down.

Understanding Love

True understanding of love is the choice that lies within the hearts of the individual. Possessed by the spirit called love. Motives are the sudden thought that inspires behavior. Actions, good or bad, it is based on one's thought. Yeah, love will do bad things once provoked, threatened or when jealous. How else can one explain the hands that cradle you, hold you, caress you are the same hands that strangle and abuse you. She poisoned him because he was cheating. He's doing time because he caught her sleeping with his friend. She angrily circumcises him for not been faithful. He abuses his spouse, she degrades him and belittles him, he yells at her, she disrespects him, etc. These are the immaturity stages of love, the war within, the deadliest stage of all transformation. Where physical abuse is the battleground to conquer the spirit called love, has transformed to hate. One who does not overcome this stage either dies or their love becomes dysfunctional. This is what we call the traits of love/ hate, the uncanny signs of love. Apprehension of this love is vital for the next stage. At this stage one will have to sacrifice their will, emotions and feelings for the en-betterment of oneself or for the sake of the union. Without love one can never know hate; without hate one can never know love. A coin with two heads is a counterfeit, likewise a coin with two tails is a counterfeit. One cannot accept love without accepting the potential to hate. Likewise one cannot embrace hate without the potential to love. The irony is which side will control you. The tail which is dominated by fear, envy, bitterness, hate, lust, anger, strives, unfaithfulness, etc. The head is dominated by peace, joy, strength, love, knowledge, faithfulness, etc. The understanding is, Love will be so much better when we surrender to each other.

Love Waiting

Last night I spoke to you. It's been a long time I said. You said you it had been a while, and that you missed me. I didn't reply, but in my mind I said I love you. You said you have to take the call waiting, so you put me on hold. While waiting I started to recollect the memories I had of you. Every moment was a delight. I love thinking about you. Your face, your smile, your teeth, your eyes, your laughter, your hands, your ears, your legs, your shape, your beauty, your mind, your talks, the way you speak and walk and act. I love everything about you. So much in awe of you, time has passed me by, with no realization that I'm trapped between your phone line waiting.

I'm Thinking of You

There's a girl I know, she knows me too.

I like her, that she does not know.

We are good friends because I act like I don't like her, But I'm very nice to her.

So nice that she misses me when I'm not around, but it hurts me too.

One day these hurts will turn to joyful feelings,

When she realizes she has feeling for me.

I wonder if she will conceal her feelings, like I'm doing. But it will hurt her

Like it's hurting me.

Who will then give in, whoever first says I'm thinking of you.

A Wishful Kiss

A kiss from you will chase my fears away.

A kiss from you will ease my pain.

A kiss from you will calm my nerves.

A kiss from you will melt my soul.

A kiss from you will make my dreams come true.

A kiss from you will satisfy me.

A kiss from you will make me happy.

A kiss from you will give me hope.

A kiss from you will make me smile.

A kiss from you will make me love you.

A kiss from you will make my day.

A kiss from you will make me blush.

A kiss from you will make me high.

A kiss from you will make me think of you.

A kiss from you will make me laugh.

A kiss from you will bring me joy.

A kiss from you will make me feel good.

A kiss from you will make me dance.

A kiss from you will make me jump.

A kiss from you will make me shout.

A kiss from you will make me sing.

A kiss from you will make me cry.

A kiss from you will make me shout.

A kiss from you will make me say "YES."

A kiss from you will make me think.

Girl, I wish I could kiss you.

How Long

How long has it been,

How long will it take,

How long will this keep going on, How long.

How long do I have,

How long do I wait,

How long do I keep trying,

How long do I love someone who don't love me back, How long.

How long will I sing,

How long will you continue to tune me out,

How long do I have before we dance,

How long.

How long will my heart feel this pain,

How long will my mind hold the memories I have of you How long, how long?

You keep running, and I'm chasing you, You keep resisting me and I'm not fighting.

I'm holding on to you, like a man hanging from a rope You push me away like you do your dog.

How long will you keep running, How long will you resist me.

How long will you keep me on hold, How long will you push me away.

How long will you deny your feelings for me,

How long will you hurt the one that loves you.

How long will you ignore my phone calls,

How long? As long as it takes till your mine.

You're in My Mind

Where can you go or where would you go.

That my love will not find you.

Where can you hide, that my love cannot uncover.

Where can you sleep without me watching over you.

You are the thoughts on my mind, the warmth I feel when I think of you. The fantasy of being with you again, and again, again, and again is ripping me apart.

Never will I give you up, never will I let you go. I love you, I need you. I will be close wherever you go, wherever you hide, I'll be there hiding to. You are my dream, the thoughts I have when I'm asleep. This is unreal, so surreal I need a reality check. You're constantly on my mind.

Intoxicated

My love for you is too much for me.

Your love is sweet, sweeter than honey.

Money is what it costs me; when I'm with you I run out of funds.

I love how you taste, how you move when you move.

Your touch makes me feel so good.

So good I lose sight, no consciousness of self or my surroundings.

Wasp in your love, your love soothes and comforts me.

I can't think straight; I wobble around you, I lose control.

You totally control me, your love is too much for me.

Your love makes me do things I don't remember.

When I look at you, your beauty, your eyes, smile and especially your breasts hunger me.

I crave for your love; your love magnetizes me. Oh when you do me, when you do the things you do to me. When you put it on me. I can't walk or talk, my legs get weak and my knees numb. I try to get up and walk. I collapse like a drunken fool. All bruised, swollen, yet I feel no pain. I'm left alone high and dry. I'm addicted to you love. I'm under the influence, I'm WWI walking while intoxicated.

Fetish

She stunted me with her beauty, her eyes gave me a cue.

Her smile okayed my approach.

My introduction was confirmed by a handshake.

Complementary on her looks was fueled by my lust for her.

The desire to have her and to hold her was strong, to love her so soon.

My eyes couldn't resist her two heresy kisses planted in her bosom. Like implants, didn't care if it was real or fake. All I know is that it was nice. I mean Nice.

My desires became intense, my mouth watery, so watery I had to lick my lips.

I wanted her more and more as we talked and walked. The conversation had nothing to do with it. But it was flowing right; she's feeling it, she feeling me.

Neither was it her look; it was a plus. It was my fetish of her.

I'm loving it, I love her, I mean her breasts, it hungers me, it's pretty, it's ripe, it look right. I like it, looks like it will melt in my mouth.

I wish I could hold her, touch it, kiss it, yeah so soon. I'm gonna ask her if I can kiss her 'cause I can't control it; these moments of instant desire are my fetish.

Foolish Love

A fool in love is like a blind man's sight. They don't see the wrong you do.

Grateful

Your picture on the wall reminds me of how beautiful you are. When I'm with you it reminds me of how fortunate I am to have a beautiful lady by my side who wants to give me her love.

Chapter 6

Love Songs

Love Has a Way

Ever since we met I haven't been the same. Ever since we touch things have not been right. It could only be right when I'm right with you. Your character forbids me. My situation prohibits us to love one another.

For now we must let go, go our separate ways. If it's love then love will find a way.

Because love has a way. (Chorus)

Because love has a way. (Chorus)

Because love has a way. (Chorus)

NO matter how far we journey from each other, nor the distances we stand apart, our love will see us through. No matter what girl or guy stands in our way, it's just to pass time. For love is infinite and it does not die.

For now we must let go, go our separate ways. If it's love then love will find a way.

Because love has a way. (Chorus)

Because love has a way. (Chorus)

Because love has a way. (Chorus)

Looking into your eyes, I see me. You looking in my eyes, you see me. I'm all you will see. You're all I need. My love grows stronger and stronger when we are apart. My love gets warmer and warmer when we are close.

For now we must let go, go our separate ways. If it's love then love will find a way.

Because love has a way. (Chorus)

Because love has a way. (Chorus)

Because love has a way. (Chorus)

I Want You to Be My Lady

We been friends for a while,

We have been looking out for each other like no other.

Our time has come, now that we both are alone.

Let us explore our friendship,

'Cause I'm feeling you.

I know you won't hurt me 'cause our friendship means a lot.

I know it hurts, for me to be putting you through this, but you want this.

It's hurting me every day that I don't tell you how I feel. That's why I'm asking.

I…want…you to be my lady, I want you to be, my girl. (Chorus)

I…want…you to be my lady, I want you to be, my girl. (Chorus)

I…want…you to be my lady, I want you to be, my girl…

I know things are gonna be different, it's gonna feel strange But I wanna take the chance.

I know we're gonna argue for the first time

I'd be cautious and always put our friendship first Because it was there when I fell in love with you.

I know you won't hurt me 'cause our friendship means a lot.

I know it hurts, for me to be putting you through this, but you want this.

I...want...you to be my lady, I want you to be, my girl. (Chorus)

I...want...you to be my lady, I want you to be, my girl. (Chorus)

Yes, it's true first friends then lovers

Yes, it's true the best love is the one you were once friends with. Yes, it's true friendship that grows will lead to love. I love you and love.

I know you won't hurt me 'cause our friendship means a lot.

I know it hurts, for me to be putting you through this, but you want this.

It's hurting me every day that I don't tell you how I feel. That's why I'm asking.

I...want...you to be my lady, I want you to be, my girl. (Chorus)

I...want...you to be my lady, I want you to be, my girl. (Chorus)

How Strong Is Your Love?

My love is weak when you're not around, I got sad,
Insecure about you and me and

What's happening to us

I need to know

How strong is your love (chorus)

How strong is your love (chorus)

How strong is your love (chorus)

Confusion has taken a hold of me

I don't know, I can't think straight

All I see is you leaving me for that man

You once loved, the one who took your virginity.

How strong is your love (chorus)

How strong is your love (chorus)

How strong is your love (chorus)

I was there for you when he broke your heart

Who wiped your tears and nursed your tender wounds?

Who came to your rescue when he left you stranded on the highway?

I need to know

How strong is your love (chorus)

How strong is your love (chorus)

How strong is your love (chorus)

Introductory to "Is It love?"

We have been going steady for a while now. The sudden death in my family altered our summer plan. I had to go away. It won't be long, as we hugged, kissed and fondled each other. We couldn't let go, 'cause what we had was special. You promise me you will wait for me no matter how long it takes. I promise you that I'll be true no matter how long it will be. So I went away. Wow, when you're in love an hour away from the one you love seems long; a day feels like forever. I did take a little longer than what we had planned but I came back home looking for you. So devastated I was to find out the love of my life had been dating someone. Once she found out I was back in town she quickly broke up with her friend. I avoided her as long as I could. Didn't answer her calls, her text messages, nor her emails, knowing good and well that I'd take her back in a heart beat. Until one day our paths crossed, when I was coming home from playing ball while she was coming home from the gym. We walk through the park; all I could think about was how I loved her and how much I missed her. She talked to me, asking me to give her a chance, asking me to look at her. I couldn't look at her; then she would see how much I love her. She kept trying to turn my face to look at her, to look into her eyes. Then her eyes were teary and she started to cry, for fear that I wouldn't take her back. That's when I broke down and sang her this song.

Is It Love?

Oh whoa whoa, oh whoa woa,

It's alright, ooooh it's alright

Dry the tears away, you are mine,

The only one someone I can call my own.

Right or wrong let it be

Isn't that what love's about?

Chorus

Is it love...tell me is it love

Is it love...darling, is it love.

I could not sleep

I toss and turn, visions of you I see Oh what's happening, what's going on Is it me, girl, I never felt like this before. Chorus

Is it love...tell me is it love

Is it love…darling, is it love.

When I look at you,

All my wonders are wonderful

I wanna hold you so close, kiss and caress you till you feel me inside you I wanna pour love, girl, on you

I'd take my time, you see.

Chorus

Is it love…tell me I'm in love

Is it love…darling, I'm in love.

I love you…baby, I love you…

I love you…baby, I love you…

What Goes Around Will Come Back Around

Baby, you said that you're

Leaving me tonight.

The look on my face is

The same look I saw

When I said to her

Bye, bye for you.

You promise me the

Moon and the stars

You told me to reach for you.

You promised me we'd "be together forever"

And ever and ever more

Just remember that

Chorus:

What goes around will come back around What you do to me will be done back to you

All your love was a lie,

Your kisses, your hugs and caresses

Were useful only for using me

For your gain, now is causing me pain.

You promise me the

Moon and the stars

You told me to reach for you.

You promised me we'd "be together forever"

And ever and ever more

Chorus:

What goes around will come back around What you do to me will be done back to you

I wish I could say go

"I hope life treats you kind."

I wish I could say

"Just call my name and I'll come running" But I can't, your love is painful.

Maybe when these hurts subside

Then I could wish you "joy and happiness"

You promise me the

Moon and the stars

You told me to reach for you.

You promised me we'd "be together forever" And ever and ever more Chorus:

What goes around will come back around What you do to me will be done back to you